SOUTHEAST COAST

PHOTOGRAPHY BY ART CARTER
TEXT BY GEORGE REIGER

GRAPHIC ARTS CENTER PUBLISHING COMPANY, PORTLAND, OREGON

International Standard Book Number 0-912856-95-5
Library of Congress Catalog Number 85-071193
Copyright © 1985 by Graphic Arts Center Publishing Company
P.O. Box 10306 • Portland, Oregon 97210 • (503) 226-2402
Editor-in-Chief • Douglas A. Pfeiffer
Designer • Robert Reynolds
Cartographer • Thomas Patterson
Typographer • Paul O. Giesey/Adcrafters
Printer • Graphic Arts Center
Bindery • Lincoln & Allen
Printed in the United States of America

To my family who tolerated my many wanderings
and to my father who, more than anyone else,
would have been proud of this book.

Art Carter

Frontisphoto: Horses found on several of the barrier islands from Assateague to
Cumberland may be descended from animals that swam ashore from shipwrecks
in earlier centuries. Horseback riding in the surf is a popular way to celebrate the
dawn at Sea Island, Georgia.

From the seventeenth century to the modern era, ships have been at the heart of history along the Southeast Coast. A sailor descends from the rigging of one of the few remaining "tall ships" which periodically visit Norfolk harbor.

Islands protect the marshes; the marshes protect the mainland. The Nature Conservancy's acquisition of more than thirty-four thousand acres of Virginia's barrier islands and fringing salt marshes has helped protect the tidal ecosystem of the entire Eastern Shore peninsula south of Maryland.

Above and overleaf: A pony grazes on Assateague Island, Virginia. Although these Assateague Island ponies resemble other horses in every respect but their smaller size, this breed is uniquely adapted for survival on salt grass and brackish water.

Above: The Cape Hatteras Lighthouse was built in 1870 and is still the tallest lighthouse in the United States. *Right:* The dunes of North Carolina attracted the Wright brothers more than eighty years ago. Today they lure enthusiasts like this hang glider at Jockeys Ridge State Park. *Overleaf:* Crested terns of several species nest on the Cape Romain National Wildlife Refuge in coastal South Carolina.

Left: White ibis settle in for the night in Beaufort County, South Carolina. Sun-warmed seas flood adjacent marshes and provide ideal conditions for many species of shallow-water fish, which in turn attract more than a dozen species of wading birds to feed and breed. *Above:* This stained glass window was designed in 1904 by Louis Comfort Tiffany for the Faith Chapel on Jekyll Island, Georgia. Tiffany was one of the wealthy people who wintered here from 1886 to 1942.

The sand dunes of Georgia's Golden Isles may be piled high one day and swept away the next, not only by the ever-present wind but also by a process called *saltation*, where individual grains of rolling sand dislodge others, making them airborne and perpetuating the movement started by the wind.

Regardless of the reasons we give for visiting the Southeast Coast—swimming, boating, sunning, surfing, fishing, birding, or just idle beachcombing — we are really there to feel the planet's pulse.

Waves rushing up the strand are heartbeats, and the twice-daily cycle of tides is the earth's respiring. The planet breathes more deeply toward the poles as though invigorated by the chilly, but extremely fertile arctic seas. By contrast, tides are barely perceptible near the equator in keeping with the languid pace of life in those transparent and largely sterile waters.

Yet from Assateague Island on the Maryland-Virginia border to Cumberland Island, Georgia, tides move with an erratic energy not unlike the lives of the millions of people who live in this diverse region. Although computerized tables predict each pulse, the tides submit to the eccentric demands of winter winds and summer breezes which add or subtract an hour here or a fathom there to previously scheduled turnings.

My love for the coast comes from conditioning as well as breeding. Every Sunday during childhood a struggle took place between my scientific father and my religious mother for the souls of their three sons, and the prize and the battlefield were beaches not far from our home. My mother always managed to get her sons to church on major holy days, but sometimes she won other Sundays as well, when my father went fishing by himself or with friends or was otherwise weary of the weekly struggle. He felt Sundays were too sacred to be spent in church, and I can still recall him striding across the sand into the full force of a northeaster with rain streaming from his hat, mustache, and rain-sodden overcoat, sermonizing that if there were a God Almighty, He was more likely to be found on a wave-pummeled beach than in a nave full of the self-satisfied.

My favorite season at the beach is the late winter or early spring, when sea temperatures are warm enough to activate fish and the birds that prey upon them, yet still cool enough to discourage swimmers and less than dedicated beachcombers. But there were always a few surfcasters scattered along the shores of my childhood, just as today there are always a few surfers resting on their boards beyond the breaking walls of water.

As I grew older, I developed a different but even more romantic view of the summer beaches. I joined the perennial line of young men and women who stroll the strand in search of dream mates. Perhaps because the sighing sea induces us to anticipate too much, we mostly pass one another by, dazzled and blinded by the light scintillating from the waves.

Older people expect less and, thereby, receive more. Their principal regret is that increasing age is a terrible price to pay for maturity. An unbroken whelk shell becomes a pleasant find; a glass fishing float, an emerald treasure. Epiphanies are seen in stranded forms of sea life, which seem to offer proof of nature's immortality and our own small roles in the drama of life. John Masefield observed that, "The hours that make us happy make us wise." Yet happiness, like wisdom, is as varied as the coastal settings which may inspire it. One of the subtle satisfactions in being near the sea is the constant reminder that man's laws are nothing compared to nature's.

As the northern hemisphere rolls back toward the sun each spring, a shade is raised all along the Southeast Coast. Increasing light and warmth pull many fish and birds north from their wintering grounds in the tropics. Terns and turtles from Cuba and Costa Rica, gulls and marlin from the Bahamas and Brazil funnel up the coast in pursuit of herring and squid which spent the cooler months in deep water beyond the continental shelf.

Everywhere, a changing of the coastal guard occurs. In South Carolina, breeding sandwich and royal terns arrive not long after wintering black-backed and herring gulls have departed. In Virginia, restless flocks of black-bellied plovers and ruddy turnstones pause on their way to the Arctic as pairs of piping plovers and willets begin their courtship rituals on the beaches and in the marshes.

One February lunch hour on Charleston's Battery, I overlooked the cloudy, breezy bay. A solitary Bonaparte's gull picked at barnacles on rubble exposed by the low tide. Four hours later when I passed by, the tide was high, and the bay was full of sunlight. The Bonaparte's gull was gone, but squads of squabbling laughing gulls dipped and soared just beyond the sea wall while three brown pelicans glided in single file toward Fort Sumter. Spring had sprung in a single afternoon.

I was born near the sea and have lived close to its pulse most of my life, but only in retrospect does my residence on the Southeast Coast seem inevitable. My father loved to explore the region by boat, and I especially remember a youthful trip to one of the tiny fishing villages that bracket Assateague Island. My older brother and I played at sailors and pirates (a coastal variation on cowboys and Indians) and armed ourselves with the telsons or tail spikes of dead horseshoe crabs found along the beach. We fished around dock pilings for black sea bass, puffers, and eels, and I still recall my father cutting skinned eels into sausage lengths and dropping them into the hot grease of a pan where they continued to twitch while frying. Unconsciously, I was being imprinted with a need to live near the ocean.

In early summer, in many bays along the coast, horseshoe crabs in countless thousands crawl inshore to spawn. Clouds of semipalmated sandpipers, sanderlings, red knots (nineteenth-century gunners called them "robin snipe"), and ruddy turnstones in breeding plumage flutter and trot around the crabs to feed on their greenish eggs. A frenzy sometimes seizes children and city visitors who cannot comprehend such immense fecundity, and as a boy of eight I would dash among the birds, grab the primordially paired crabs from the sucking sands, and hurl them into deeper water. If the crabs had not finished spawning, they would simply crawl back into the shallows to fulfill their ancient mandate.

One still summer day, I heard the explosive gasp of a respiring sea turtle and saw an enormous loggerhead clutching a horseshoe crab in its huge parrotlike beak. The crab's telson pivoted helplessly for a moment before the turtle crushed the crab and sank with its prey beneath the surface of the sea. My father explained that just as the shorebirds feed on horseshoe crab eggs, the marine turtles feed on the crabs, and the sharks in turn feed on the turtles frequently found napping at the surface of the sea. The birds, crabs, turtles, and sharks have all lived on earth for tens of millions of years—far longer than we, with our capacity to make food, fertilizer, oil, ornaments, and even weapons (Indians used horseshoe crab telsons as arrowheads before my brother and I used them as play swords) from every other creature. This information percolated through my youthful brain, and a vision emerged of myself and other people as part of nature and, simultaneously, as giants and dwarfs within it.

Human history came to fascinate me as much as the natural kind, and when I moved into secondary school it became increasingly clear that American history, even such a narrow band of it as that encompassed by the Southeast Coast, is incomprehensible without a study of other histories: European history, at least as far back as Greek mythology; African history, back at least to the black man's first contact with whites; and early Asian history, from the time the first Indians came to the New World. As I studied, I found that what little was known about life along the Southeast Coast three centuries ago intrigued me more than all the rest of America's past. The character of a new breed of humanity was then beginning its evolution on the shores of the lower Chesapeake, and the pride and independence of the Indian, the law and industry of the European, and the endurance and compassion of the African were meeting in pristine isolation and creating a culturally innovative subspecies known as the *American*.

Although the English eventually established colonies all along the Southeast Coast, the Spanish had been there many times before, teaching the natives much about the *realpolitik* which accompanies European law and industry. In 1610, settlers on the James River met an Indian chief whom they called Powhatan after one of the more than two hundred towns which paid him "eight parts of ten tribute of all commodities which their country yieldth, as of wheat, pease, beanes ... skyns, and furrs." Historians are almost certain that such large-scale tribute was never paid among the pre-Columbian Algonquin tribes found from coastal Carolina to Labrador and that such unique exploitation possibly was inspired by a local Indian kidnapped by the Spanish in 1561. Christened Don Luis de Velasco and educated in the uses of terror and torture for achieving political ends, Don Luis returned to the Chesapeake in 1570 with a party of Jesuit priests. He had learned his lessons from his Spanish mentors so well that he promptly murdered the missionary party and returned to his family—possibly Powhatan's own—where he served as an advisor in the ways of the white man.

A century later, when the English settled Savannah near a Creek village called Yamacraw, the British found the Indians so bitterly familiar with the Spanish that as soon as Chief Tomochichi learned the British were mortal enemies of Spain, he swore his allegiance to England. Since Georgia initially banned slavery, the local Creeks helped the colonists to build their town and to hunt down Spanish soldiers encamped on the coastal islands, and after the ultimate victory over the Spanish at Bloody Marsh on June 9, 1742, the Creeks adopted the kilted clothing worn by the Scottish Highland regulars. Ironically, this costume came to be depicted as the "authentic" dress of the Creek, Cherokee, and Seminole nations.

Everywhere you travel along the Southeast Coast, you will find traces of mankind's most daring political experiment and meet the ghosts of many people you would like to have known. Jamestown's will to survive gave way to Williamsburg's urge to prevail, and, a little over two hundred years ago, each of the southern colonies joined their brethren to the north in saying "Enough!" to Britain's paternalism. Yet in order to understand General Oglethorpe in eighteenth-century Georgia, you must also comprehend Governor Berkeley in seventeenth-century Virginia. And to admire fully the success of Washington, Jefferson, and Patrick Henry, you must know of the valiant failure of Nathaniel Bacon, William Drummond, and Richard Lawrence in 1676.

The world is too well explored today for young people to know the opportunities and risks, the freedom, and the amazing bounty of the *new* New World which our ancestors shared. Yet if we peel back the layers of plastic found along much of the modern Southeast Coast, we may still see—in a Jacobean chimney, a nesting tern, an old basket, a surf fisherman, or an arrowhead picked from a freshly plowed field above a salt marsh—the continuity beneath the exaggerated changes wrought by superficial technology.

My wife, son, and I live in an eighteenth-century farmhouse on land that was deeded in the seventeenth century and hunted over by people for thousands of years before that. The sea that twice daily licks the foundations of the road running across the marsh beyond my front door is still rising. The best scientific predictions say that sea levels along the Southeast Coast will be a foot higher within the next thirty to fifty years and as much as five feet higher by the end of the next century. In fact, the Atlantic Ocean is now rising at a rate more than three times faster than during the previous three thousand years, when the seashore lay a good many miles east of its present perimeter. Since the front stoop of our farmhouse is barely ten feet above current sea level, my farm is certain to be reclaimed by the ocean in the not distant geological future.

That knowledge is curiously reassuring. It reminds me that continuity is still the foundation of change, that dawn still follows dusk, that death, as Shakespeare wrote, is only a "necessary end" to life. Just as the nurturing soils of my farm will be nurtured—with bobwhite quail calling from hedgerows bordering newly planted corn, whistling mourning dove wings flaring over soybean stubble, Canada geese grazing on emerald fields of winter wheat—the soils of my farm will nurture and be nurtured by wildlife, until the Eastern Shore is once again returned to the sea. So my soul is nurtured by ideas and ideals planted in ages past, which I bequeath to others even as I write.

Hope, despite our knowledge of inevitable death, is what distinguishes our species from all others and touches us with divinity. Ambition and experience are the sunlight and rain which inspire our souls to flower. Yet if seeds are cast upon barren ground, the few that germinate will wither, for only a knowledge of human and natural history provides the fertility in which the human psyche can flourish.

My wife and I each traveled widely, lived abroad, and married late in our initially independent and, later,

A reproduction of the Susan Constant *is moored at Virginia's Jamestown Festival Park. The original held seventy-one people.*

Waterside, which houses shops and eateries along the Norfolk waterfront, is one of the city's most popular tourist attractions.

mutual quest for Shangri-la. We found our haven on the Southeast Coast through a process of elimination which accepted the fact that the small world we hoped to protect in perpetuity with our deed of trust was already changing. Thus, our love of history is not only the sextant by which we set our future course, but the consolation and keel stabilizing us today.

My wife and I continue to explore the Southeast Coast, even though we feel in harmony with our home and possessive of the diminishing days we have to share it. We have a seven-year-old son who wants to see worlds we have seen, and although these worlds are greatly changed, they are worlds he must know to acquire his own touchstones of understanding. When we set off on a trip, I frequently pack a guide from the past to help me cope with the present. For the Southeast Coast, Nathaniel H. Bishop's *Voyage of the Paper Canoe* cannot be excelled. Between 1874 and 1875, Bishop paddled and rowed a fifty-eight-pound paper canoe from Troy, New York, to Cumberland Island, Georgia. The southern stretch of his expedition makes for the most memorable reading, and in a ceremony ending his trip on the *Maria Theresa* in St. Mary's, Georgia, Bishop thanked his Southern friends for making the trip possible:

> The oystermen and fishermen living along the lonely beaches of the eastern shore of Maryland and Virginia; the surfmen and lighthouse keepers of Albemarle, Pamplico, and Core sounds in North Carolina; the ground-nut planters who inhabit the uplands that skirt the network of creeks, marshes, ponds, and sounds from Bogue Inlet to Cape Fear; the piney-woods people, lumbermen, and turpentine distillers on the little bluffs that jut into the fastnesses of the great swamps of the crooked Waccamaw River; the representatives of the once powerful rice-planting aristocracy of the Santee and Peedee rivers; the colored men of the beautiful sea-islands along the coast of Georgia ... all have contributed to make the "Voyage of the Paper Canoe" a success.

However, this was all after the fact. In the autumn of 1874, Nathaniel Bishop was not at all sure of the welcome he would get in the former Confederate states, or even whether he would make it down to the warmer Carolinas before winter set in. On Friday, November 27th, he crossed the border into Virginia and arrived at Chincoteague as night was falling:

> The ebb-tide had left but little water around the rough pier abreast of the town, and heaps of oyster-shells rose from the mud flats and threatened the safety of my canoe. I looked up through the darkness to the light pier-head above me, and called for assistance. Two men leaned over to inquire: "What's the row now, stranger?" To which I replied, "I wish to land a light boat on your pier; and as it is made of paper, it should be carefully handled." For a moment the oyster men observed a silence, and then, without one word of explanation, disappeared. I heard heavy boots tramping up the quay towards the tavern. Soon a low murmur arose on the night air, then hoarse shouts, and there came thundering down the wharf an army of men and boys.

> "Pass her up, stranger!" they cried. "Here, give us your bow and starn painters, and jest step overboard yourself, and we'll hist her up." Some of the motley crew caught me by the shoulders, others "histed away," and the canoe and its captain were laid roughly upon the ground.

> There was a rush to feel the paper shell. Many were convinced that there was no humbug about it; so, with a great shout, some of the men tossed it upon their shoulders, while the rest seized upon the miscellaneous cargo, and a rush was made for the hotel, leaving me to follow at discretion and alone. The procession burst open the doors of the tavern, and poured through the entrance to a court-yard where they laid the boat upon a long table under a shed, and thought they had earned "drinks." This was the spontaneous way in which the Chincoteague people welcomed me.

Chincoteaguers still spontaneously welcome strangers, particularly if they suppose the strangers can render favors in return. On one of our flounder-fishing trips out of Captain Bob's skiff livery in Chincoteague in the 1960s, Barbara and I caught twenty-two flounder, including an 8½ pounder, in three drifts and quit because that was all we and our friends at home could possibly use. When we got back to the dock, the proprietor greeted us like prodigal children, had me sign up for a state citation, and even took several pictures of Barbara and myself holding the doormat-sized fish.

"Mighty nice of you to go to all this trouble," I said.

"What trouble?" he replied. "When this picture gets in the local paper, I'll have two dozen fishermen down here trying to catch a bigger one!"

Chincoteaguers are a clannish lot, even today, and just as most residents of the Eastern Shore are content with our separation from the rest of the Commonwealth of Virginia, Chincoteaguers like the channels which separate them from the rest of Accomack County. Unfortunately, bad as well as good results from this attitude. The good is that Chincoteague watermen are among the most self-reliant people I have ever known; the bad, that they are among the most insular and know and care little about the rest of the world only a few miles away.

Nathaniel Bishop discovered this trait one hundred years ago when he tried to get directions for the channels south:

> Of all this community of watermen but one could be found that night who had threaded the interior watercourses as far as Cape Charles, and he was the youngest of the lot. Taking out my note-book, I jotted down his amusing directions. "Look out for Cat Creek below Four Mouths," he said; "You'll catch it round there." "Yes," broke in several voices, "Cat Creek's an awful place unless you run through on a full ebb-tide. Oyster boats always has a time a-shoving through Cat Creek," &c. After the council with my Chincoteague friends had ended, the route to be travelled the next day was in my mental vision "as clear as mud."

Such renowned Chincoteague decoy carvers as Ira Hudson and Doug Jester had not yet been born when Nathaniel Bishop made his coastal odyssey. But one man in the crowd milling about Bishop, and possibly even the young man who knew something about the channels to the south, could have been decoy carver Dave Watson. Watson, who died in 1938, was so little known and appreciated in his day that the most distinctive thing locally remembered about this supreme craftsman is that he frequently carried a bumbershoot, which earned him the sobriquet, "Umbrella."

Chincoteague was joined to the mainland by a long causeway in 1922, and a bridge joining Chincoteague to the barrier island, Assateague, was completed in 1962. This event, more than the advent of the causeway, finally brought Chincoteaguers into the mainstream of peninsula life. With the bridge came tens of thousands of visitors each year to see the birds at the National Wildlife Refuge, to swim at the National Seashore, and to watch the "wild ponies."

Bishop observed that these "hardy little animals," which are found at intervals along the beaches down to the sea-islands of the Carolinas, are called "Marsh Tackies." He wrote:

The inhabitants of [Chincoteague] are not all oystermen, for many find occupation and profit in raising ponies upon the beach at Assateague, where the wild, coarse grass furnishes them a livelihood. . . . They hold at Chincoteague an annual fair, to which all the "pony-penners" . . . bring their surplus animals to sell. The average price is about ninety dollars for a good beast, though some have sold for two hundred and fifty dollars. All these horses are sold in a semi-wild and unbroken state.

The Chincoteague herd is all that is left of the many scattered herds which once roamed the barrier islands of the Southeast Coast. They had proved to be unprofitable, a nuisance to people with lean lifestyles once the automobile appeared, so they were rounded up and sold, mostly for food. The Chincoteague herd escaped this fate due to its unique role in the local economy.

Every July, the horses, which are smaller than most breeds but larger than a Shetland pony, are swum across the channel separating Chincoteague from Assateague, where they live most of the year. At Chincoteague, a designated surplus is auctioned off amid much fanfare and mythology about how the progenitors of the herd escaped from the wreck of a Spanish galleon four hundred years ago.

Although Chincoteague's "marsh tackies" have been around since at least the eighteenth century, their gene pool has been refurbished periodically by other horses. A few years ago, when equine encephalitis wiped out a major portion of the herd, "adopt-a-horse" mustangs were shipped in from federal lands in the west. These animals were not adapted to a diet of salt grass and had great difficulty adjusting to the presence of both people and seasonal clouds of mosquitoes and green-head flies. Some of them attacked visitors, and the local volunteer fire department, which manages the herd, resolved not to repeat the experiment.

The most notable fact which emerges from a comparison of Bishop's commentary on the horses with the current pony-penning scene is that the prices for the animals are almost the same today as they were in the 1870s — which means that the real price of a horse has diminished enormously. Although a record price of $1,250 was bid for a Chincoteague pony in 1980, that is still less than the $250 paid in 1870. However, the volunteer fire department is content with the money it receives, since its overhead is not high, and the local town boosters are ecstatic, for some pony-penning weekends bring in so many visitors and tourist dollars that shopkeepers can close up and vacation further south in the winter.

Bishop stayed only overnight in Chincoteague before continuing down the coast. He wandered into one cul-de-sac in the marsh the next morning, but managed to get out and cross two inlets safely. He stayed the night with a farmer named Martin R. Kelly, whose descendants still farm on the mainland to the west of Gargathy Inlet. The following night, near Wachapreague, he stayed with Captain William F. Burton. Nearby Burton Bay took its name from this family. Captain Burton told his guest that lobsters were occasionally taken on hook and line in Wachapreague Inlet. Since there are no rocky reefs or ledges in nearby waters, these were most extraordinary catches. An Eastern Shore lobster fishery exists today, but the lobster boats run more than forty miles out to sea to set their pots.

A modern dredged channel would have enabled Bishop to paddle directly to Hog Island, but in 1874 he had first to paddle back out to Wachapreague Inlet where a storm almost swamped his canoe. He finally made it to a large marshy island just inside the inlet:

I leaped out and drew my precious craft away from the tide, breathing a prayer of thankfulness for my escape from danger, and mentally vowing that the canoe should cross all other treacherous inlets in a fisherman's sloop.

Bishop camped there, but was kept awake all night by the scratching of curious raccoons and muskrats and the quacking of ducks. A decade later, a local hunting fraternity erected several buildings and a cistern for freshwater near Bishop's campsite. Renaming the island Clubhouse Marsh, the Accomac Shooting Club headquartered there and was active into the 1920s.

Today, only a portion of the old cistern can be seen at the north end of the island at low tide, and even the high ground where the clubhouse stood, and where a heron rookery existed until the early 1970s, is subsiding into the bay. However, blackducks, muskrats, and raccoons still use the area, and, a decade ago, an otter stole one of my teal decoys, left out overnight in one of the island's saltwater ponds.

The next morning Bishop passed down the length of Parramore Island, which he said was "called Palmer's by the natives." I suspect that Bishop, a Yankee, was not yet used to southern accents — especially the Eastern Shore variety — which easily make "Palmer" out of Parramore. Bishop then passed Hog Island, and, because its famous shooting club did not yet exist, he hardly mentioned the now vanished town of Broadwater "within a forest of pines." The club brought the town a brief prosperity around the turn of the century, but this ended before World War I. When the hurricane of '36 knocked the stuffings out of what was left, most residents abandoned Hog Island to the sea birds and a small crew of the Coast Guard. Although a new lifesaving station was built in the 1950s, it was sold as "government surplus" not long after completion for a fraction of its cost to a group who turned it into a private duck club. The rest of the island, along with most of the Virginia Eastern Shore barrier island chain, is now owned by The Nature Conservancy — and tens of thousands of nesting water birds.

It is odd that Bishop did not spend more time at the next island, for not only was Cobb already a major resort in the 1870s, but the man for whom the island was named and whose sons then ran it was a Massachusetts man like Bishop himself. However, their families hailed from different sides of the track, and Bishop perhaps believed that Cobb Island was already too well known to need description. Since the resort catered mostly to wealthy Yankees, Bishop may have felt that the hostel was not sufficiently reclusive to justify much space in his diary. Whatever the reason, he stayed an undescribed overnight. The next day:

> ...in company with the regular row-boat ferry I crossed...the broad bay to the mainland eight miles distant, where the canoe was put upon a cart and taken across the peninsula five miles to Cherrystone, the only point near Cape Charles at which a Norfolk steamer stopped for passengers.

Nathaniel Bishop did not feel comfortable in Norfolk. For the first time in his voyage, he was entering what had been enemy territory only ten years earlier, and he may have been uncertain of his reception. The Union Army had occupied the Eastern Shore so early in the Civil War that no fighting had occurred, which is the principal reason so many lovely colonial homes remain. But Norfolk was a different matter, and until he left the city, Bishop kept a decidedly low profile.

At least he tried to keep a low profile. Unfortunately, he met one of those local newspaper reporters unable to distinguish between publicity and journalism. Tracking Bishop down to his lodgings, this young man from the *Norfolk Landmark* practically dragged him out of bed.

> "Mr. Bishop," proclaimed the reporter, "you are a man of snap. We like men of snap; we admire men of snap; in fact, I may say we cotton to men of snap, and I am proud to make your acquaintance. Now if you will stop over a day we will have the whole city out to see your boat."

Horrified at the prospect, Bishop bid a hasty adieu to Norfolk shortly after breakfast. However, just as Bishop deserved better treatment, Norfolk deserved better than his brief reference to its "dismantled hulks lying at anchor in the stream [and occupying] both banks of the river." Like any hardworking entity, city or sailor, Norfolk has too often been given a bum rap.

In a more reasonable world, nearby Virginia Beach would be a borough of Norfolk, since so many people who work in Norfolk reside there. Suburbanized and highly subsidized, home to most of the military personnel in the Norfolk area, Virginia Beach could provide Norfolk with the tax base which it so desperately needs to flourish.

But despite their separation, Norfolk has managed to prevail. Twenty years ago, it was a tarnished city. The downtown area suggested it had been on the loser's side in World War II rather than the western Atlantic's most important staging area for victory in North Africa and Europe. The federal government has appreciated Norfolk's strategic importance, and through a variety of federal programs has refurbished the downtown Waterside district and added the Scope Convention Complex and a World Trade Center. This physical transformation has encouraged a can-do spirit equally stimulating to Hampton, Newport News, and Portsmouth.

The route that Bishop took south from Norfolk matches in many stretches the Intracoastal Waterway authorized by Congress forty-five years later. Although the entire system now stretches all the way from Gloucester, Massachusettes to Brownsville, Texas, it was first conceived as a southeastern coastal barge canal to help get the still stagnant Southern economy moving. The Army Corps of Engineers — which built and maintains the waterway — used as many natural rivers in the coastal plain and bays behind the barrier island chain as it could to speed development of the system and to cut construction costs.

About six miles from Norfolk, wrote Bishop:

> The entrance to the Dismal Swamp Canal is reached, on the left of the [Elizabeth] river. This old canal [which dates back to colonial times] runs through the Great Dismal Swamp, and affords passage for steamers and light-draft vessels to Elizabeth City, on the Pasquotank River, which empties into Albemarle Sound to the southward. The great cypress and juniper timber is penetrated by this canal, and schooners are towed into the swamp to landings where their cargoes are delivered.

Bishop was now entering one of the first regions of the Southeast Coast to be explored by British colonists and one of the last to be developed by their descendants. George Washington helped survey the Dismal Swamp which, despite its name, is a place of great mystery and beauty. Drummond Lake lies in the middle of this vast, wetland forest, and even today, as in Bishop's day, "bears are found in [its] fastnesses."

It is a pity that Bishop did not have time to poke around. In December, Drummond Lake is blanketed with rafts of ring-necked ducks, and bald eagles feed there on sick or crippled wildfowl and on its great concentration of largemouth bass. Unusual for a swamp lake, Drummond does not act as a sump into which water flows from the surrounding land. On the contrary, water is constantly flowing out of Drummond Lake to the sea. This fact makes for a most pleasant conclusion to a day spent exploring the lake by canoe, as I did a decade ago with a party of friends. The current is with you as you head for the highway and home.

The canal system directing the waters of the Dismal Swamp to the sea were dug, as Bishop put it, "in the old days of the wheelbarrow and spade," in order to drain the region and to reach timber needed by the British Navy and later by our own maritime fleets. Its present 330 square miles represent less than one-third its pre-colonial size.

Juniper, alias white cedar, a lightweight yet durable wood ideally suited for spars and booms, complemented the white pine hulls once fashioned from New England forests. Although cypress is the east's most weather-resistant wood, and at least as durable as redwood, it was too splintery to be used for hulls or decking by the navy since cannon fire was one of the hazards of warfare aboard wooden ships. However, cypress still is used to make durable workboats ranging from skiffs and scows to Chesapeake Bay skipjacks. It also was used to make window frames and doors for early American homes, and I fancy the large paneled doors that open into our kitchen were cut from Dismal Swamp cypress some time in the early nineteenth century.

Bishop records that:

> About noon, I arrived at the Locks of the Albermarle and Chesapeake Canal. The telegraph operator greeted me with the news that the company's agent in Norfolk had telegraphed to the lock-master to pass the paper canoe through with the freedom of the canal—the first honor of the kind that had fallen to my lot.

Bishop was relieved and delighted by the friendly reception he received almost everywhere in former Confederate territory. When he reached Pungo Ferry, he met Charles N. Dudley, a southern gentleman who offered every inducement in his power to persuade northern men to settle in the vicinity. Bishop knew, of course, that it was not "northern men" so much as their relative wealth and energy which were wanted and desperately needed. Ten years after the Confederacy had drafted the last white males between fourteen and fifty-six years of age, the region still had not recovered its pre-war population. Many coastal citizens owned hundreds of acres but could not acquire the capital and labor needed to work their holdings. While some farmers in North Carolina hung on and continued to work the land by themselves or with a handful of blacks willing to sharecrop, Bishop would discover in South Carolina that tens of thousands of acres of rice fields had been abandoned by landowners who knew that such labor-intensive farming would never again be profitable, unless machinery could be invented to do the work that slaves had done.

Among the services rendered by Bishop's journey for modern geneologists are his brief sketches of the people he meets. Unlike other areas of the country, the people who first settled the Southeast Coast have continued to frame its history. Until the 1950s, fresh ripples of immigration were always small enough to be absorbed by established families. The name *Dudley*, for example, has long been found in the records of the Virginia-North Carolina coastal counties. Even while Bishop was paddling down the Pasquotank River, two thirteen-year-old boys, Lee and Lem Dudley, were hunting and carving birds not far away on Knotts Island. The decoys, especially the ruddy ducks and canvasbacks made by the brothers, are today among the most beautiful and most sought-after wooden birds in the world.

Another large service provided by Bishop's profiles is the admiration we come to feel for the simple dignity of the people he meets:

> It was almost dark when I reached the storehouse at Pungo Ferry; and as Sunday is a sacred day with me, I determined to camp there until Monday. A deformed negro held a lease of the ferry, and pulled a flat back and forth across the river by means of a chain and windlass. He was very civil, and placed his quarters at my disposal until I should be ready to start southward to Currituck Sound.

Professional golfer Jan Stephenson competes at Moss Creek Plantation at Hilton Head, South Carolina.

Ferris wheels and other wild rides accommodate thousands of thrill seekers during Myrtle Beach's Sun Fun Festival.

That night, after a sparse dinner and a cup of yaupon tea, the "good-natured freedman" told Bishop his story:

He had too much ambition, he said, deformed as he was, to be supported as a pauper by the public. "I can make just about twelve dollars a month by dis here ferry," he explained. "I don't want for nuffin; I'se got no wife — no woman will hab me. I want to support myself and live an honest man."

Yaupon, the drink "that cheers but not inebriates," was the principal form of liquid refreshment along the Southeast Coast before the advent of bottled soft drinks. Unfamiliar with it, Bishop wrote:

This substitute for the tea of China is a holly.... It is a handsome shrub, growing a few feet in height, with alternate, perennial, shining leaves, and bearing small scarlet berries. It is found in the vicinity of salt water, in the light soils of Virginia and the Carolinas. The leaves and twigs are dried by the women, and when ready for market are sold at one dollar per bushel. It is not to be compared in excellence with the tea of China...

However, North Carolina wines can be compared with Europe's. John Lawson — a founder of New Bern and surveyor general of North Carolina in 1708 — was murdered by Indians in 1711. Before he died, he distinguished six varieties of native grapes found in North Carolina, including the Scuppernong, the Catawba, and the Isabella. The Scuppernong grew on the banks of the Scuppernong stream, whose mouth is near the eastern end of Albemarle Sound. Of the six varieties, five were discovered in Tyrrel County by Philip Amadas and Arthur Barlow. Tradition relates that these sixteenth-century explorers carried one small vine to Roanoke Island, where it may still live.

Bishop was impressed by the quantities of waterfowl he saw at Currituck and he understood that what attracted the birds was the large brackish water impoundment that Currituck Sound had become since the natural closing of the inlet forty years before. The consequent growth of brackish and sweet-water plants drew wildfowl which in turn drew "northern sportsmen." Bishop observed that, "The best 'gunning points,' as in the case of Chesapeake Bay, are owned by private parties, and cannot be used by the public."

He also noted that swans were the wariest of all the waterfowl, "not permitting the canoe to approach within rifle range." Captain Peter L. Tatum, the proprietor of Bell Island, explained to Bishop how the great birds were obtained:

"It is hard work to get hold of a swan, though they are a large bird, and abundant in Currituck Sound. You must use a good rifle to bring one down. After a strong norther has been blowing, and the birds have worked well into the bight of the bay, near Goose Castle Point, if the wind shifts to the south suddenly, gunners approach from the outside, and the birds becoming cramped in the cove are shot as they rise against the wind."

The swans of the Southeast Coast are native tundra or whistling swans which breed in Alaska and the Yukon and concentrate each winter from the Chesapeake to Mattamuskeet Lake, a national wildlife refuge since 1934. Swans are long-lived and slowly maturing birds which were overshot by market gunner and recreational shooter alike. Since American sportsmen frown on the shooting of any gamebird with a rifle, they petitioned the federal government, which has ultimate responsibility for the management of migratory birds through a number of treaties with Canada and Mexico, to prohibit the use of rifled ammunition for wildfowling and to protect the swan.

That was sixty-five years ago. Today, the continental population of tundra swans has substantially increased and they are a nuisance to farmers, especially those trying to grow winter wheat. In 1984, North Carolina initiated a carefully regulated swan season in which 1,000 hunting permits for a single bird each were distributed through a lottery. Despite the assumption of many non-hunters that swans would be easy to shoot after so many years of protection, the permit holders seem to agree with Captain Tatum that it is hard work, especially with a shotgun.

Bishop's canoe was fitted with oarlocks so he could vary his means of locomotion and he rowed down Currituck Sound one enjoyable morning:

Gunners were passed, secreted behind their 'blinds,' or pens of pine brush, which looked like little groves of conifera growing out of the shoal water. Geese were honking and ducks were quacking, while the deep booming of guns was heard every few minutes.... [live] decoy-birds were anchored in many places near the marshes. Every sportsman gave me a cheering word as the canoe glided over the smooth water, while here and there the violet-backed swallow darted about over the marshes as though it were summer.

Bishop was impressed by the maritime forest behind the dunes north of Nag's Head. "On this high beach," he wrote, "the hills were well covered with yellow pines, many of which were noble old trees." The local Baptist minister, Hodges Gallup, owned much of this area. "His domain extended for several miles along the beach, and, with deer quietly browsing in his grand old woods, formed a pretty picture."

Nag's Head itself impressed Bishop as "desolate," "dreary," and "forlorn." However, he might have been thinking as much about its rumored reputation as the land he actually saw. The people of Nag's Head took their livings from the sea, but not all the work was the honest labor of haul-seining striped bass and flounder in the surf or harpooning dolphins in the sound to render them down for oil. The people of Nag's Head were also wreckers. This should mean that they merely salvaged ships driven ashore by storms, but darker traditions have it that the men often lured ships onto the beach with false signals from lanterns slung from the necks of the horses which they walked along the high dunes behind town.

Whether true or not, Bishop was happy to push on to his next destination, Bodie Island Lighthouse, beckoning ten miles away. Not long before the start of his expedition, Bishop had received from an old friend and mentor, Spencer Fullerton Baird, then both the U.S. Commissioner of Fisheries as well as the Assistant Secretary (and later Secretary) of the Smithsonian Institution, "a talisman which must open any light-keeper's door." It was a letter from the Secretary of the Navy directing all lighthouse keepers to provide shelter and other assistance, when necessary, to Nathaniel H. Bishop. So Captain William F. Hatzel, whom Bishop characterizes as "a loyal North Carolinian," welcomed the weary traveler to his newly constructed (1872) lighthouse and home on Bodie Island, which Bishop spelled as it is correctly pronounced, *Body*.

> *Looking eastward, a limitless expanse of ocean; gazing westward, the waters of the great sound, the shores of which were low marshes miles away. Below me could be heard the soft cackle of the snow goose,…which had left its nesting-place on the barren grounds of arctic America, and was now feeding contentedly in its winter home in the shallow salt-ponds; [while] the gentle shur-r-r of the waves softly broke on the strand. Above, the star-lit heavens, whose tender beauty seemed almost within my grasp.*

Thanks to his lighthouse pass, Bishop discovered one of the rare pleasures of the Southeast Coast. With its low country and the surrounding sea, any kind of elevated view on a barrier island is a treat. In this century, because of their sturdy construction and the elevated panoramas they offer, lighthouses are choice properties whenever they pass into private ownership. Bodie Island, Cape Hatteras, and Cape Lookout lighthouses remain active, yet they have been automated and no longer need keepers. Bald Island Light, at the mouth of the Cape Fear River, has been decommissioned and has a private "keeper" family living there today.

As Bishop proceeded on toward Hatteras, he noted that the barrier island he passed had "once [been] heavily wooded; but the wind had blown the sand into the forest and destroyed it." He also noted that "a wind-mill in each village raised its weird arms" and was the means by which local communities obtained fresh water.

So long as local populations remained small, fresh water was relatively easy to come by on the Outer Banks. Increasingly more difficult to find, however, was driftwood for home heating and cooking once sail began to give way to fossil-fueled steel ships. Furthermore, improved navigational aids in the past half century all but eliminated the kinds of shipping disasters that were regular winter events when Bishop traveled down the coast. So, as barrier islands became increasingly unstable due to gradually rising seas and the loss of maritime forests under shifting sands, the federal government began acquiring these dynamic shores. As a result, most of North Carolina's barrier beaches now cater both to visiting birds and people.

At Kitty Midget's Hammock, today part of the Pea Island National Wildlife Refuge, Bishop stayed with Captain Abraham Hooper. The names Midget and Hooper are deeply imbedded in Outer Banks history. In my own personal history, E. Burgess Hooper saved my younger brother's life and mine on a wildfowling expedition to the area in 1963. In a similar sense, Captain Hooper saved Bishop:

> *I had drawn my boat into the sedge to secure a night's shelter, when the old captain on his rounds captured me. The change from a bed in the damp sedge to the inside seat of the largest fireplace I had*

> *ever beheld, was indeed a pleasant one. Its inviting front covered almost one side of the room. While the fire flashed up the wide chimney, I sat inside the fireplace with the three children of my host, and enjoyed the genial glow which arose from the fragments of the wreck of a vessel which had pounded herself to death upon the strand.*

Bishop and his host spent the next day netting in the surf for bluefish. The large eight to thirty-pound bluefish go south as far as Cape Hatteras and then disappear into deep water far offshore; the smaller editions stay inshore and eat their way down the Southeast Coast to Florida, accompanied by great flocks of scavenging gulls.

Although Bishop is awed by the vast expanses of sand and water he finds as he paddles down the Banks, although he ends up pushing himself through as much shoal water as he paddles through, he clearly feels at home with the Bankers and their precarious ways of eking out a living.

Not a great deal was to change over the next century. A story I heard as a youngster described a party of visiting anglers marveling at how well local people lived without the benefits of a more complex society.

"What do you do about disputes without lawyers and courts?" asked one angler of a Banker who had helped provision the party.

"We let the preacher settle it," replied the Banker.

"How do you protect your property without a sheriff or police?" asked another fisherman.

"We know all the thieves," replied the Banker, "and it doesn't make any difference."

"How do you handle influenza and broken bones?" asked the doctor in the party.

"We patch 'em up with spar splints or rub 'em down with pneumonia cure and feed 'em all a little East Lake licker. They get well."

"Don't tell me," said the exasperated physician, "that no one ever dies here!"

"Oh, yes. They die. Fact is, fellow died just two weeks ago."

"Aha!" said the doctor triumphantly. "Now won't you admit that if you had had a physician, he might have saved the poor fellow's life?"

"Nope," said the Banker. "Fact is, the fellow drowned, and we ain't found his body yit."

Bishop himself must have worried a little about drowning as he made the last leg to the cape. He quoted the old refrain, "Hatteras has a blow in store for those who pass her howling door," and described the interesting way he got there:

> *Before proceeding far the wind blew a tempest, when a young fisherman in his sailboat bore down upon me, and begged me to come on board. We attempted to tow the canoe astern, but she filled with water, which obliged us to take her on board. As we flew along before the wind, dashing over the shoals with mad-cap temerity, I discovered that my new acquaintance, Burnett, was a most daring as well as reckless sailor. He told me how he had capsized his father's schooner by carrying sail too long. "This 'ere slow way of doing things," he detested. His recital was characteristic of the man.*
>
> *"You see, sir, we was bound for Newbern up the*

Neuse River, and as we were well into the sound with all sail set, and travelling along lively, daddy says, 'Lorenzo, I reckon a little Yaupon wouldn't hurt me, so I'll go below and start a fire under the kittle.' "Do as you likes, daddy," sez I. So down below he goes, and I takes command of the schooner. A big black squall soon come over Cape Hatteras from the Gulf Stream, and it did look like a screecher. Now, I thought, old woman, I'll make your sides ache; so I pinted her at it, and afore I could luff her up in the wind, the squall kreened her on to her beam-ends. You'd a laughed to have split yourself, Mister, if you could have seen daddy a-crawling out of the companion-way while the water was a-running down stairs like a crick. Says he, ruther hurriedly, 'Sonny, what's up?' "It isn't what's up, daddy; but what's down," sez I; "it sort o'looks as if we had capsized.' 'Sure 'nuff,' answered dad, as the ballast shifted and the schooner rolled over keel uppermost. We floundered about like porpoises, but managed to get astride her backbone, when dad looked kind of scornfully at me, and burst out with, 'Sonny, do you call yourself a keerful sailor?' "Keerful enough, dad," sez I, "for a smart one. It's more credit to a man to drive his vessel like a sailor, than to be crawling and bobbing along like a diamond-back terrapin." Now, stranger, if you'll believe me, that keerful old father of mine would never let me take the helum again, so I sticks to my aunt at the cape.

Bishop loved Cape Hatteras. Its restless energy was a macrocosm of his own:

The Gulf Stream, with its river-like current of water flowing northward from the Gulf of Mexico, in its oscillations from east to west frequently approaches to within eighteen or twenty miles of the cape, filling a large area of atmosphere with its warmth, and causing frequent local disturbances. The weather never remains long in a settled state. As most vessels try to make Hatteras Light, to ascertain their true position, &c., and because it juts out so far into the Atlantic, the locality has become the scene of many wrecks, and the beach, from the cape down to Hatteras Inlet, fourteen miles, is strewn with the fragments of vessels.

Although there are fewer wrecks to see today, a major storm will scour out the beach and move the dunes so that old tragedies come to light again. The hurricane of 1944 uncovered the hull of the ghost ship, *Carroll A. Deering*, out of Bath, Maine, which was found on Diamond Shoals in 1921, with sails set, with uneaten food on the table and on the stove, but with only a cat to greet the Coast Guard crew which boarded her.

Also exposed by the '44 storm was the British tramp, *Ariosto*, which foundered in 1899. Twenty-one of her men were buried in the dunes outside Ocracoke, but six survived, including one sailor who swam ashore with a fruitcake in a tin can. The fruitcake was served on Christmas Day to the other survivors and the Coast Guardsmen who had helped save them, and since it was the very first fruitcake ever seen on the Outer Banks, it is better remembered today than the name of the sailor who brought it.

Maritime tragedies inspired maritime heroism, and in no other area on earth have so many Congressional Medals of Honor been earned. Twenty-seven men have been honored on the Outer Banks "in the name of Congress for conspicuous gallantry and intrepidity at the risk of life above and beyond the call of duty." In both World Wars I and II, Coast Guardsmen braved storms and burning seas, sometimes under fire from German submarines, to rescue sailors from dying ships.

On August 8, 1918, a German submarine attacked the Diamond Shoals lightship. Captain W. L. Barnett and his crew fought back with small arms until their ship began to go under. They then escaped by rowing twelve miles to the beach. Eight days later, Captain John Allen Midgett and five members of the Chicamicomoco Coast Guard Station made several trips through seas of blazing oil to rescue forty-two men from the British tanker, *SS Mirlo*, torpedoed by a nearby German sub.

Thanks to Mother Nature and the German Navy, there was so much metal lying on the bottom in this Graveyard of the Atlantic after both world wars that for many years the compasses of passing ships were pulled off north by as much as eight degrees. But even iron and steel are consumed by the sea, and after forty years of relative peace, both from European politics and Caribbean-spawned hurricanes, fewer wrecks and less magnetic metal are today found near Cape Hatteras than at any time in the past two hundred years.

When Bishop arrived at Hatteras, he found a letter from Judge I. E. West of the yacht *Julia*, out of New Bern, which had been cruising for a week between Roanoke Island and Ocracoke Inlet in order "to capture the paper canoe and to force upon its captain the hospitality of the people of that city." Bishop decided to spend Christmas with the gentleman who sent this charming message, but first he had to cross Hatteras Inlet. This was not as simple as it sounds. Bishop was in a state of high anxiety:

Upon entering the swash I thought of the sharks which the Hatteras fishermen had told me frequently seized their oars, snapping the thin blades in pieces, assuring me, at the same time, that mine would prove very attractive, being so white and glimmering in the water, and offering the same glittering fascination as a silver-spoon bait does to a blue-fish.

About midway across, Bishop was suddenly surrounded by rambunctious denizens of the deep and nearly had heart failure. Fortunately, he quickly made the happy discovery that his companions were porpoises and only old acquaintances.

Bishop had endured much skepticism as he paddled or rowed down the coast. But his canoe had never before suffered such indignities as those it endured in New Bern where a crowd tested its hull with their pocket knives. Bishop soon was eager to be back among working watermen who would not dream of harming another man's craft, and by January 6, 1875, despite a cold rain, he was happily ensconced in the village of Swansboro on Bogue Sound, where men made their livings by shipping pickled and dried mullet roe to Wilmington and Cincinnati. The many retirees who live on Bogue Sound today, some still fond of hunting, would be surprised to know of the profitable market gunning once conducted there. In Bishop's time, canvasbacks, called raft-ducks, sold from twelve to twenty cents each; Canada and snow geese brought forty cents; and brant, thirty.

Two days later, Bishop was in Topsail Sound, planning to camp in an old boathouse, when he was discovered and brought to a plantation home by the owner's son. North Carolina was then the third largest peanut producing state in the nation after Virginia and Tennessee, and Bishop's hosts, the McMillans, grew peanuts on their estate. They were extremely gracious to Bishop:

> *The family went to the landing to see me off, and the kind ladies stowed many delicacies, made with their own hands, in the bow of the boat. After rowing a half-mile, I took a lingering look at the shore, where those who four days ago were strangers, now waved adieu as friends. They had been stript of their wealth, though the kind old planter had never raised his hand against the government of his fathers. This family, like thousands of people in the south, had suffered for the rash deeds of others.*

Throughout his sojourn in the Carolinas, Bishop was to hear the same refrain. When he stopped near Mason Inlet at the plantation of Captain Mosely, "late of the Confederate army," the Captain's hogs greeted Bishop in a friendly fashion and then the Captain himself with the words, "The war is over, and any northern *gentleman* is welcome to what we have left."

At Mason Inlet, Bishop determined he would have to bend inland by wagon to Wilmington and take the train to Flemington, on Lake Waccamaw, where he would follow the Waccamaw River back to the sea at Georgetown and Winyah Bay.

Of Wilmington, Bishop wrote practically nothing. This is odd considering the town's importance during the Civil War when, because of its relatively inland location, it was the last Confederate port to be closed by federal troops and the Union blockade. Today, Wilmington is not only North Carolina's largest port— receiving petroleum products and shipping tobacco, wood products, and scrap metal—the city is a rail hub, a resort, and a recreational fishing center. Thanks to an excellent artificial reef-building program run by the state, the relatively barren near-shore waters now concentrate great quantities of game fish. Several summers ago, I enjoyed a particularly memorable morning over a carefully sunken hull within sight of the hotels and condominiums lining Wrightsville Beach. In addition to catching several king mackerel and having half-a-dozen amberjacks break my line in the reef, I landed a citation-sized Spanish mackerel.

With such immensely valuable timber on all sides of Bishop, it seems peculiar to us that the only forest-related industry in the upper Waccamaw drainage during this period in the late nineteenth century was the extraction of pitch, tar, and turpentine from the pines that grew on the scarce high ground. Yet North Carolina is known as the Tar Heel State precisely because the very resinous but scraggly pines that flourish in the sandy soils of its coastal plain have always been better for the production of turpentine than for lumber.

Bishop launched his canoe on the Waccamaw and quickly declared it to be "this most crooked of rivers." The first day he sped downstream some twenty miles in

Tankers cruise past a window on Factors Walk and the Cotton Exchange, landmarks along Savannah's River Street.

Whitney Lake, a tannic-stained blackwater pond, is part of the wilderness of Cumberland Island, Georgia.

three hours—yet found he was still only four miles, as the heron flies, from where he began. It took him another day of paddling to reach South Carolina, where he found large-scale cypress logging operations in contrast to the pitch, tar, and turpentine distilleries he had passed upstream. Although Bishop had company in the form of raftsmen, he missed the coast with its clear definitions of distance. No two "lumbermen, ignorant or educated, would give the same distance," he reported, and he yearned to meet anyone for whom the word *miles,* statute or nautical, meant something.

Conwayborough, as it was called in the nineteenth century, was the principal town in northeastern South Carolina. It boasted a railway and shipped cotton and naval stores to the north after barging the commodities nine miles down the Waccamaw to Pot Bluff. This place, reported Bishop, "is reached by vessels from New York drawing twelve feet of water." Much of the original Waccamaw was incorporated into the Intracoastal Waterway, and the region's principal town today is Myrtle Beach. Myriads of visitors play each summer on the thirty-five miles of sand stretching between North Myrtle Beach and Murrells Inlet where, in Bishop's day, only loggerhead turtles came ashore to spawn.

As Bishop paddled down the Waccamaw, he stayed alternately with black and white families who were most solicitous of his welfare, but from very different points of view. The blacks looked after him because he was a "good man, capt'n—we knows dat." And when Bishop asked them how they knew that, they replied, "Cause you couldn't hab come all dis way in a *paper* boat if de Lord hadn't helped you. *He* dono help only good folks."

The white Crackers, so called, says Bishop, "because they subsist largely upon corn," looked after him because they viewed Bishop as an innocent in a land of thieves and cutthroats and were horrified to learn that he had already stayed among blacks. Bishop had to endure many tales of fear and suspicion about blacks from whites. On balance, he may have preferred the simple faith of his occasional black hosts.

As Bishop descended the Waccamaw, he saw a culture that was already moribund. Near Conway he found that, "though still a long distance from the ocean, I was beginning to feel its tidal influences." Some thirty-five miles from the sea, the Waccamaw and her sister stream, the Pee Dee, were delayed by tides, a fact which enabled coastal South Carolina to become, as early as the mid-eighteenth century, the most productive per-acre rice-producing region in the world. The tides backed up the fresh-water rivers into a complex system of canals, dams, and flashgates allowing planters to drain and flood their fabulously fertile lowlands.

Bishop saw his first rice plantation, Tip Top, twenty-two miles below Pot Bluff, where Bull Creek enters the Waccamaw from the Pee Dee River. He paddled up Bull Creek in order to visit Bates Hill Plantation, then the home of M. L. Blakely of New York who had come south to supervise "the labors of his four hundred freedmen in the swamps of North and South Carolina." The same blacks who had provided the know-how and labor to operate huge rice plantations now worked as loggers and shingle-makers.

Charles Joyner in his recent book, *Down by the River-side,* points out that not only was the first seed rice introduced to South Carolina from Madagascar, but "...the early technological knowledge [of rice culture] was supplied by Africans, not Europeans. ...While over the years the Europeans contributed their engineering and management skills to extending and rationalizing the system of rice cultivation developed by the Africans, striking continuities between African and Afro-Carolinian methods of planting, hoeing, winnowing, and pounding (dehusking) the rice persisted through slavery and on into recent years."

Because Carolina planters sought slaves with rice-growing experience, the slave markets of Charleston featured men and women from Senegal-Gambia and the Gold Coast who mixed their blood with the Congo-Angolans who had entered the colony in the 1730s. Today, a distinctive black culture called Gulah still exists along the South Carolina coast and into Georgia. There is a quiet racial pride among Carolinian blacks found in few other regional black populations outside Africa, because the Carolinians know their roots. Although they were born the sons and daughters of black chattel, they are the grandsons and granddaughters of the Mandingo or Fullah, Gola or Guinea, Yoruba or Ibo, Fante or Ga, and they know that the wealth and prestige which once belonged to South Carolina would not have been without their knowledge and labor.

Bishop did not understand the black's indispensable role in rice culture, and he did not realize that freed blacks were interested only in producing enough rice to feed themselves, while slave blacks had to produce a surplus to make their owners rich. Consequently, he writes:

The paper canoe had now entered the regions of the rice-planter. Along the low banks of the Pee Dee were diked marshes where, before the civil war, each estate produced from five thousand to forty thousand bushels of rice annually, and the lords of rice were more powerful than those of cotton, though cotton was King. The rich lands here produced as high as fifty-five bushels of rice to the acre, under forced slave labor; now the free blacks cannot wrest from nature more than twenty-five or thirty bushels.

This was indeed a sorrowful, if inevitable, chapter in the history of a region which had placed too many of its prosperous eggs in the basket of slavery. Long gone was that romantic era when the French Marquis de Lafayette and the German Baron de Kalb arrived on the shores of South Carolina to pledge do-or-die allegiance to the cause of American Independence. Gone were the nights Francis Marion, "the Swamp Fox," rested his men in hiding from British troops at the rice plantations of his in-laws, the Allstons. Gone, too, were the triumphal tours of presidents: first Washington, who in 1791 stayed at Brookgreen and Clifton plantations; then Monroe, who visited Prospect Hill in 1819; then Van Buren, who became an honorary member of Georgetown's distinguished Planters Club in 1842.

Although labor-intensive rice culture faded in the Carolinas, the rice fields themselves became increasingly attractive to wintering wildfowl. And wealthy Yankees or Southerners like Bernard M. Baruch, who had gone north to make their fortunes, bought some of the old plantations where they entertained guests or business clients. Grover Cleveland became the first president to visit South Carolina after the Civil War when, in 1894, he fell overboard while hunting ducks on a coastal plantation, and during the 1940s Winston Churchill and Franklin Delano Roosevelt visited Baruch at the Hobcaw Barony. Between discussions of world events, Churchill fished; Roosevelt, hidden by a blind, shot ducks from his wheelchair.

Bishop passed through Winyah and Bull bays and entered Charleston one evening when the lateness of the hour reinforced the mystery and melancholy of his surroundings:

The gloomy mantle of darkness was settling over the harbor as the paper canoe stole quietly into its historic waters. Before me lay the quiet bay, with old Fort Sumter rising from the watery plain like a spectral giant, as though to remind one that this had been the scene of mighty struggles. The tranquil waters softly rippled a response to the touch of my oars; all was peace and quiet here, where, only a few short years before, the thunder of cannon woke a thousand echoes, and the waves were stained with the life-blood of America.

Bishop was prepared to sneak in and out of town, but the enthusiastic greeting he received from the black postmaster made this impossible. Then, before he could return to his quarters at Mount Pleasant, members of the Chamber of Commerce, the Carolina Club, and others, pressed their "kind attentions and hospitalities" upon him, and the *Maria Theresa* was displayed on the Southern Wharf.

When the first Confederate shell fell on Fort Sumter in April, 1861, Charleston's many attributes became tarred by the brush of war, and modern visitors are frequently as astonished as Nathaniel Bishop by the contrast between the city's belligerent reputation and its hospitable reality. Founded in 1680, Charleston quickly developed into the most important port in southeastern North America, exporting indigo, rice, and deerskins. Three hundred years later, Charleston is still one of the most important ports in the southeastern United States, exporting fertilizer, chemicals, steel, asbestos, cigars, pulp, paper, textiles, and clothing. It is also headquarters for the Sixth U.S. Naval District and for the U.S. Air Force Defense Command.

Charleston's charm, however, stems not from her industries, but from the creative uses to which her residents have long put their leisure time. After the Dock Street Theatre opened in 1736, arts and letters became important ingredients of Charleston's life, including such oblique participation as Cabbage Row, which became Catfish Row in DeBose Heyward's novel *Porgy*. Science and education were important to Charleston even before Dr. Louis Agassiz lectured at the medical college during the winter of 1851-52. In addition to this school, known now as the Medical University of South Carolina, the city is home to the Citadel, to the Baptist College at Charleston, and to the College of Charleston, which dates back to 1790 and in 1837 became the first municipal college in the nation.

Charleston has an Old World flavor which distinguishes it from other cities of the Southeast Coast. The Anglo-Saxons, French Huguenots, Caribbean Celts, and European Jews who founded and developed the city gave it a cosmopolitan flair and religious tolerance still evident in modern Charlestonians. Unfortunately, their success and clannishness also gave the city a rigid social hierarchy, which was based on the date when a family could boast it had arrived. Such snobbery is rapidly eroding as new money and new attitudes percolate through the community.

When Bishop left Charleston he was entering a navigational no-man's land, for no survey had been completed for the coast south of the city. He stayed one night with former Governor William Aiken on Jehossee Island, but not long after leaving Aiken's plantation with its grounds of magnolias and live-oaks, he became lost in the marsh. To make matters worse, a fog came in from the sea so that Bishop lost all sense of direction. Finally, miraculously, he discovered a huge ship, anchored in a tidal river, which was the erstwhile royal yacht of the Russian emperor and was now a Finnish freighter, the *Rurik*, picking up a load of phosphates. With new directions from the ship's captain, Bishop set out the next morning for Chisolm's Landing, near Beaufort.

This town, pronounced "Bewfort" to distinguish it from North Carolina's Beaufort, was originally established by the English as a buffer outpost between their indispensable trading center at Charleston and the Spanish, French, Indians, and pirates foraging to the south. Beaufort was barely settled in 1710 when its first residents fled due to a war with the Yemassee Indians, and, despite the protection of its first fort in 1717, the town was not incorporated until 1803.

Beaufort was the center of secession sentiment in South Carolina, which led to the Civil War and then to the decline of the rice empire between the Grand Strand and Charleston. As a result, Beaufort emerged as the center of the sea-island cotton industry and profited more after the abolition of slavery than during any decade before the war.

In 1663, Captain William Hilton usurped a century-old French claim to the island that bears his name. However, Hilton Head did not become historically important until 1861, when thirteen thousand federal soldiers, sailors, and marines landed there to establish headquarters for the Union's Department of the South. It was here that the Yankee blockade of the Atlantic Coast was directed. After the war, although Hilton Head and the other sea islands along the southern Carolina and Georgia coasts contributed to the enhancement of cotton as King, time and history seemed to pass them by. This, at least, was the way Nathaniel Bishop found Hilton Head when he arrived there in 1875 and bivouacked with its sole resident, a Mr. Kleim, formerly of the First New York Volunteers and the only military man among the original thirteen thousand who remained after the war. Kleim, who lived in an old store near one or two even more ramshackle buildings, sold a little merchandise and did a little farming. Rather pretentiously, he called his "estate" Seabrook Plantation.

Seventy-five years after Bishop's visit, Hilton Head was still largely deserted. Then four men formed the Hilton Head Company and began lobbying to have a bridge built to join the island to the mainland. The bridge was completed in 1956, and the development stampede began. The Sea Pines Plantation Company split off from the original Hilton Head Company, and, in 1968, an old hunting estate was turned into Palmetto Dunes, the third major development on the island. It is doubtful that Nathaniel Bishop would recognize Hilton Head Island today — or any of the other developed sea islands of South Carolina and Georgia. But Bishop certainly would be able to find better amenities than those he encountered in Mr. Kleim's kitchen, where he dried his canoe's meager cargo.

As Bishop entered "the broad, yellow, turbulent current of the Savannah," he did not think of General James Edward Oglethorpe's master plan for the city upstream, or the destruction it suffered during the Revolution and narrowly missed during the Civil War. Rather, Bishop remembered the voyage of the *Savannah*, the first steamship ever to cross the Atlantic. She left her namesake city on May 25, 1819, and reached Liverpool, England, on June 20th. But this adventure was nothing compared to the one the people of Savannah believed Bishop was undertaking. Most were woefully ignorant of geography and insisted that he had come from Canada "over the Atlantic Ocean," and Bishop could not convince them that he had rarely been out of sight of land.

Because Savannah, unlike Charleston, had escaped the worst effects of the recent war, and because cotton, unlike rice, could be cultivated profitably with paid labor, the golden years of Savannah's history still lay ahead when Nathaniel Bishop visited the city in 1875. The reason for the daily swelling population of Irish and German immigrants were the many new jobs in construction and shipping. Abraham Lincoln had understood the commercial mentality of Georgia's port city when he learned in the closing months of the war that captured Savannah was already bustling with business: "I reckon they'll accept the situation," observed the President, "now that they can sell their cotton."

My wife, Barbara, was born in Savannah. Her great-grandfather came to the city after the Civil War to capitalize on a boom which rivaled anything in the American West. Although a man might work as a fisherman supplying food to the city, or as a railroader as Barbara's grandfather did, every Savannahian, directly or indirectly, served King Cotton. At its peak in the 1890s, the city was shipping more than two million bales a year aboard nearly two thousand ships.

Like any people who experience a bonanza, Savannahians saw no reason to change a thing—no reason to diversify their economy or to develop manufacturing interests possibly inimical to King Cotton. So when the British decided to limit their purchases of cotton to what their expanding colony in Egypt produced, and too much American cotton found too few markets, the bubble burst. For nearly half a century, the town shrank, and Savannah was left with its lovely parks, gracious homes, and memories.

World War II was a period of renewed growth, as Savannah's shipbuilders worked overtime to provide the Allied fleets with Liberty ships. My wife's mother christened one of these, the *Arlie Clark*, but she was sunk less than eighteen months later by a German submarine.

After the war, Savannah diversified its economy to include chemicals, petroleum, rubber, lumber, plastics, and paper as well as shipping. By the mid-1960s, the city was sufficiently affluent to begin doing something about the remark made to a local reporter by Lady Nancy Astor ten years earlier. She had said, "Savannah looks like a beautiful woman with a dirty face! Why don't you get a mop and clean her up?" Well-heeled retirees, younger craftspeople, and shopkeepers soon combined forces to create still other local growth industries: historic restoration and the tourist trade it inspired.

Bishop was eager to push on to Cumberland Island and the St. Mary's River where he would leave the coast and end his journey. He took notes while drifting downstream:

Leaving Greenwich, Bonaventure, and Thunderbolt behind me on the upland, the canoe entered the great marshy district of the coast along the Wilmington and Skiddaway rivers to Skiddaway Narrows, which is a contracted, crooked watercourse connecting the Skiddaway with the Burnside River. The low lands were made picturesque by hammocks, some of which were cultivated.

The next day, he entered the Great Ogeechee through the Don Island passage and saw sturgeon fishermen at work with their nets along the shores of Ossabaw, one of the sea islands.

Since Atlantic sturgeon are a slow-growing and late-maturing species (the females may not begin breeding until they are fifteen years of age), they are rapidly overfished whenever a local spawning population is discovered. This was true in Virginia's tributaries of the Chesapeake in the eighteenth century, of North Carolina's and Georgia's river mouths in the nineteenth century, and of the sturgeon fishery which was promoted by South Carolina's Wildlife and Marine Resources Department and quickly collapsed in the 1970s.

Bishop found the weather delightful when he passed the deer-abundant forests of Ossabaw Island. Had he possessed a light tent:

I would not have sought shelter at night in a human habitation anywhere along the route. The malaria which arises from fresh-water sinks in many of the sea islands during the summer months [a salt-marsh variety of mosquito can also carry malaria and yellow fever], did not make camping-out dangerous to the health.

His next stop along the Georgia Coast was High Point on Sapelo Island:

From among the green trees of the high bluff a mansion, which exhibited the taste of its builder, rose imposingly. This was, however, but one of the many edifices that are tombs of buried hopes. The proprietor, a northern gentleman, after the war purchased one-third of Sapelo Island for fifty-five thousand dollars in gold. He attempted, as many other enterprising northerners had done, to give the late slave a chance to prove his worth as a freedman to the world.

... He built a large mansion, engaged his freedmen, paid them for their work, and treated them like men. The result was ruin, and simply because he had not paused to consider that the negro had not

*been born a freedman, and that the demoralization
of slavery was still upon him.*

In all the decades since Bishop left Sapelo, the island has changed little, thanks to the fact that much of it was donated decades ago to the University of Georgia, which uses it for marine research. Here many of our most important concepts about the workings of the salt marsh were first deduced and tested.

There was a new warmth and languor in the sea air that Bishop greatly enjoyed and which persuaded him to stay for several days on Broughton Island with Captain Richard A. Akin, one of the few men after the war to have made a success of rice planting with wage-paid labor. The difference seems to have been one of personality, for Bishop says of Akin that, "...the negroes seemed to like their employer, and stuck to him."

The next major island Bishop visited was St. Simons, "where Mr. Pierce Butler once cultivated sea-island cotton, and to which he took his English bride, Miss Kemble." However, the plantation was almost abandoned and Bishop continued alongside the island on the Frederica River until midway, where he paused to survey what remained of the old town of Frederica.

*History informs us that Frederica was the first
town built by the English in Georgia, and was
founded by General Oglethorpe.... The fortress
was regular and beautiful, and was the largest, most
regular, and perhaps most costly of any in North
America of British construction.*

Oglethorpe's extravagance was tolerated by the Royal treasurers because the Spanish in Florida, not the French in Canada, were considered the more serious threat to Britain's valuable and vulnerable colonies in the Carolinas and the Caribbean. A reformer and philanthropist as well as a general, Oglethorpe's attributes both enabled him to found the colony and to lose his authority once his bans against rum and slavery and his advocacy of Methodism were perceived by the Crown as barring the way to further development.

Bishop, pursuing his journey southward, entered the exposed area of St. Simon's Sound:

*Its ocean inlet, was easily crossed to the wild and
picturesque Jekyl Island, upon which the two bach-
elor brothers Dubignon live and hunt the deer,
enjoying the free life of lords of the forest. Their old
family mansion, once a haven of hospitality, where
the northern tourist and shipwrecked sailor shared
alike the good things of this life with the kind host,
was used for a target by a gunboat during the late
war, and is now in ruins.*

Bishop visited Jekyll Island ten years before its development as a winter retreat for fabulously rich American families like the Goodyears, the Rockefellers, and the Macys. By 1900, the members of the Jekyll Island Club boasted that they represented one-sixth of the world's wealth. By 1942, however, their children were inclined to view the ostentation of Millionaires Village with more embarrassment than pride, and the club was closed. The State of Georgia bought this white elephant in 1947 for $675,000, a price that local boosters call a bargain, "akin to the purchase of Manhattan Island," but which insiders looked on as the cleverest deal since the first Eskimo was persuaded to buy a refrigerator. Today, Jekyll

Great blue herons and a dozen other wading species stalk their prey in Savannah National Wildlife Refuge's marshes.

Many of the beautiful homes located on Charleston's Battery are fine examples of antebellum architecture.

Island and neighboring Sea Island and St. Simons Island are worth millions of dollars in residential and resort facilities. Whether your passion is playing eighteen holes of golf on a new course each day of the week, visiting historical landmarks, or just relaxing on a beach with the prospect of superb dining to follow, Georgia's Golden Isles satisfy every hope and expectation.

Eagerly pushing on, Nathaniel Bishop missed the mouth of Jekyll Creek and after an eerie confrontation with an alligator —"the brute's head was a long as a barrel; his rough coat of mail was besmeared with mud, and his dull eyes were fixed steadily upon me"— he camped on Jointer Hammock with its cheerful owner, R. F. Williams. That night the winds turned sour, and, anxious that he would be "shut up by bad weather," Bishop prevailed upon his host to take him and his canoe across St. Andrew's Sound to High Point of Cumberland Island:

> His little sloop was soon under way, and though the short, breaking waves of the sound, and the furious blasts of wind, made the navigation of the shoals disagreeable, we landed quietly at Mr. Chubbs' Oriental Hotel, at High Point, soon after noon. Mr. Martin, the surveyor of the island, welcomed me to Cumberland, and gave me much information pertaining to local matters.

Bishop arrived during one of those wistful interludes in the history of Cumberland, which was symbolized by the rise and ruin of the various manor houses called Dungeness. The first of these dates back to Oglethorpe's day, when his military regulars played hide-and-seek with Spanish soldiers among the coastal islands. After the victory at Bloody Marsh, Oglethorpe's Scottish officers decided to commemorate their control of the Golden Isles with a hunting lodge on Cumberland which they called "Dungeness."

In 1783, the new state of Georgia gave General Nathanael Greene the best part of Cumberland's thirty-six thousand acres after a hard-nosed contractor forced the General to sell all his other estates to honor personal pledges he had signed during the American Revolution in an effort to obtain supplies for his campaigns. Somewhere near the earlier hunting lodge, Greene began erecting a four-story building of brick and tabby, a kind of concrete made of sand, lime, and oyster shell. When he died at age forty-four, his widow, Catherine, finished the home with her new husband, the plantation manager. Here they entertained the likes of Eli Whitney and Light-Horse Harry Lee. The latter died at Dungeness and was buried there until a committee of Virginians asked that he be dug up and moved north, next to the grave of his son, Robert E. Lee.

This Dungeness, gutted by fire during the Civil War, was the ruin Bishop saw during his 1875 visit. However, ten years later a third Dungeness was erected in the place of the other two by Scotsman Thomas Carnegie, brother of Andrew, the founder of U.S. Steel. His three-storied structure was topped by an Italianate cupola and surrounded by forty other buildings, including a carriage house, greenhouse, smokehouse, icehouse, and a "playhouse," which was not so much for theatricals as for squash, billiards, and indoor swimming. The estate was barely completed when Carnegie, age forty-two,

died. His widow, Lucy, never remarried, and Dungeness was only reopened once after her death for a family wedding and reunion. Then, one night in 1959, vandals burned it down with all its furnishings.

Today, Lucy Ferguson, granddaughter of Thomas and Lucy Carnegie, lives in a tin-roof house once occupied by one of her grandparents' hired hands. Although she was educated in boarding schools, traveled abroad, and had, as people used to say, "all the advantages," Lucy Ferguson knows that Cumberland Island is her home and she never has wanted to live anywhere else. A few other people still occupy holdings on the island, but half of Cumberland is now administered by the National Park Service and most of the other half, including the tidal marshes and "submerged lands," is owned by the State of Georgia.

A friend once characterized Wilderness as "anywhere I can't take my car." Cumberland is a National Seashore pointing north along a necklace of wind-cut islands to the first jewel of the Southeast Coast, Assateague. Of the four national seashores of the Southeast Coast, three of them, Assateague, Cape Hatteras, and Cape Lookout, can be reached by automobile, one way or another, and none of them offers a federally designated Wilderness Area. But there are no visitors' automobiles on Cumberland Island, and this small fact alone enables Cumberland National Seashore to encompass eight thousand acres of uppercase Wilderness.

Although some people might prefer that all our barrier islands be returned to wilderness, and others want nothing from the merger of sea and shore but amusement parks and revolving lights at night, the Southeast is unique among all American coasts in offering the entire spectrum of people's longing for the sea, from luxurious development to unbridled wilderness. The Southeast Coast provides something for everyone.

Yet that "something" is invariably linked to the sea. There would be no condominiums at Myrtle Beach without the beach, and Cumberland is all the more precious for straddling the sea and tidal marshes. Nathaniel H. Bishop sensed the essentiality of this link even as he departed from it:

> The next morning the canoe left the high bluffs of this beautiful sea island so filled with historic associations, and threaded the marshy thoroughfare of Cumberland and Brickhill River to Cumberland Sound. As I approached the mouth of the St. Mary's River, the picturesque ruins of Dungeness towered above the live-oak forest of the southern end of Cumberland Island. It was with regret I turned my back upon that sea, the sounds of which had so long struck upon my ear with their sweet melody. It seemed almost a moan that was borne to me now as the soft waves laved the sides of my graceful craft, as though to give her a last, living farewell.

The flat-bottomed Chincoteague scow is not a glamorous workboat but she does a reliable job harvesting crabs, oysters, and clams from the fertile marshes and mud banks of Virginia. Often fashioned from white cedar, such hulls sit out the year around. Humid weathering makes their joints more watertight.

Cumberland Island, Georgia. Windblown sand is the Southeast Coast's engineer and artist. It is also an enemy when dunes migrate into maritime forests and roll entire islands over on themselves so that trees found growing on the bayside by one generation are discovered in the ocean surf by the next.

More than twenty-two miles of roadless barrier beach and wilderness dunes lie between the two developed access points to Assateague Island. Straddling the border between Maryland and Virginia, the island is home to both a national seashore and a national wildlife refuge.

Oyster shells are piled ready for planting into nearby bays so that young oyster spat will have hard surfaces to settle on in order to perpetuate the cycle of growth and harvest for which Chincoteague has long been famous.

A mud-spotted face and an optimistic grin are trademarks of the Virginia water-man. Bill Spence of Wachapreague has been working the seaside marshes for over half a century, as did his great-grandfathers.

Whether low tide comes at dawn or dusk, the Eastern Shore waterman must be there to mine the exposed flats for clams and oysters. Some work with double-clawed gaffs, some employ basket-shaped iron rakes, and still others use nothing more than their feet and hands to "tread them up."

Above: Leaving fields of corn stubble and winter wheat, a flight of Canada geese returns to roost on a barrier island. *Overleaf:* Ships entering the Chesapeake from the south must round Cape Henry (in the background) and follow the narrow Thimble Shoal Channel. They sail over one of two tunnels which link seventeen miles of highway spanning the mouth of the bay.

A young black-backed gull crouches in a Virginia seaside marsh near the nest where it hatched. With almost a six-foot wingspan, this large predator is expanding its breeding range down the Southeast Coast.

Above: The smooth marshmallow *(Hibiscus militaris)* is a wildflower characteristic of the brackish and sweet-water marshes of the Southeast Coast. It was quickly adopted by eighteenth century gardeners and is still found in tidewater Virginia's Colonial Williamsburg. *Overleaf:* A laughing gull *(Larus atricilla)* at Assateague National Seashore. In April these common coastal birds return from wintering in the Caribbean to breed on Virginia's barrier islands.

Hopkins & Brother, on the bayside of the Eastern Shore of Virginia, is the oldest active steamboat ticketing agency in the mid-Atlantic. Today, in addition to selling general merchandise and summer excursion tickets to Tangier Island, the store serves as a gourmet restaurant where one can enjoy exotic cheeses and wines while overlooking boaters and watermen on Onancock Creek.

The first building on Virginia Beach, the Seatack Lifesaving Station, was built in the early 1880s. Today, twenty-eight miles of hotels and recreational facilities cater to the many thousands of visitors who delight in swimming, sunbathing, surfing, fishing, beachcombing, and jogging at dawn.

Above: The two counties of Virginia's Eastern Shore grew affluent a century ago by providing early-season vegetables for northern markets. Today, the area still grows potatoes, tomatoes, and snapbeans, but most cleared land produces wheat, corn, and soybeans. *Right:* Williamsburg's Bruton Parish Church has been in continuous use since 1715. Many prominent delegates, including Thomas Jefferson and Patrick Henry, worshiped here when the House of Burgesses was in session.

Left: James Fort provides visitors with impressions of life in seventeenth-century Virginia, before Williamsburg succeeded Jamestown as capital in 1700. *Above:* Carter's Grove, built for one of "King" Carter's sons on a site overlooking the James River, was carved out of the family's three hundred thousand-acre estate. Supposedly, George Washington and Thomas Jefferson were both rejected by early loves in the plantation's parlor, later known as the Refusal Room.

Williamsburg's Duke of Gloucester Street runs from the College of William and Mary through Merchants Square to the restored capitol and past some of the finest examples of British colonial architecture in North America.

Busy Hampton Roads encompasses three hundred and sixty years of maritime history from the first tentative explorations of Captains John Smith and Christopher Newport, through the battle between the Civil War ironclads, *Monitor* and *Merrimac,* to the modern ocean-going vessels built or repaired at the Newport News Shipbuilding and Dry Dock Company, the largest shipyard on earth.

As part of the successful effort to revitalize downtown Norfolk, the cultural and convention center known as Scope opened in 1971 and became the focus of an eight-block development featuring nearly one thousand hotel rooms, dozens of retail shops, and a free "trolley" connecting them all.

Above: Norfolk's annual Harborfest was enhanced the year of the city's tricentennial celebration in 1982 by an international fleet of square-riggers, clippers, and other "tall ships" from both sides of the Atlantic. *Overleaf:* Despite the intense development surrounding a revitalized Norfolk, tourists or working water people do not have far to go in the Chesapeake country to find themselves alone on some part of the tidal estuary, and at peace with the world.

Nearly half-a-million residents and visitors participate each June in Norfolk's Harborfest. Speedboat races, tugboat "ballets," concerts under the stars, fireworks, and sound-and-light spectacles are all part of the annual extravaganza.

Norfolk is proud of its present and in love with its past. The skipper of this craft admires the great naval ships around him, even as the sailors aboard the different warships admire his antique brigantine.

Above: Foreign visitors to tidewater Virginia, such as the crew of Portugal's naval training ship, *Sagres,* can always count on enthusiastic demonstrations of traditional southern hospitality. *Right:* Norfolk's World Trade Center is one of several federally financed redevelopment projects on the water's edge, site of the founding of Norfolk more than three hundred years ago.

Left: One way or the other, aboard mighty warships or pleasure boats, the people of Portsmouth have always followed the sea. *Above:* The importance of shellfish to the commercial and recreation history of Virginia's Eastern Shore is reflected in place names for the small towns of Clam and Oyster. From Cherrystone Creek, a tributary of the Chesapeake, "Cherrystone clams" have been shipped by railroad since late in the nineteenth century.

A lesser yellowlegs in Chincoteague National Wildlife Refuge. The refuge is an important waystation for most species of eastern North America's waterfowl and shorebirds and for tens of thousands of visitors who come to see them.

Merchants Mill Pond and some of the other lily-filled backwaters near Elizabeth City are uncharacteristic of the rest of North Carolina's coastal plain. Conversely, Currituck Sound's broad expanse of grassy flats is renowned for its largemouth bass fishing and wildfowling.

Wright Brothers National Monument. The sand dune known as Kill Devil Hill moved nearly half a mile between 1903—when Orville and Wilbur Wright made their historic first flight from its crest—and 1929, when it was anchored with a costly planting of grass and capped by this sixty-foot-tall granite pylon.

Above: The U.S.S. *North Carolina* is permanently berthed across the Cape Fear River from downtown Wilmington. This World War II veteran now serves as an educational and historical monument. *Overleaf:* The upper Outer Banks have been a surf fisherman's mecca ever since the first Tin Lizzies began bringing anglers to this remote strand more than sixty years ago.

A guide aboard a tender on Pamlico Sound sets out strings of decoys for a party of diving-duck hunters. The brackish bays between North Carolina's mainland and the Outer Banks have provided sporting recreation for well over a century. Some visitors were first brought here as boys by their grandfathers, who in turn had been brought to Pamlico as boys by their granddads.

Above: When this structure at Mattamuskeet was a water-pumping station, its tower was a smokestack. After the facility was turned into a hunting camp, the tower was capped and painted to resemble a lighthouse and is preserved today as a historical monument by the National Park Service. *Overleaf:* Sunrise on Cape Lookout National Seashore. The seashore extends sixty miles along the coast from Ocracoke Inlet on the southeast to Beaufort Inlet on the southwest.

Pea Island National Wildlife Refuge was created in 1938 to protect a prime wintering area of the gravely depleted greater snow goose. Today, *Chen caerulessens hyperborea* numbers in the hundreds of thousands and provides birding and recreational hunting opportunities for thousands of visitors to the Outer Banks.

Above: Mattamuskeet means "dry dust" in the language of the Indians, who hunted over its peaty soil. Unsuitable for early farmers, the land was flooded and is now a fifty thousand-acre sanctuary for such wintering wildfowl as Canada geese and tundra swans. *Overleaf:* A pied-billed grebe surfaces in a pond in the Croatan National Forest near the Cherry Point Marine Corps Air Station.

According to legend, Nags Head takes its name from shore-based pirates who hung lanterns around horses' necks and then walked the animals up and down the high dunes to lure unwary sailing ships onto the beach.

Since 1870, when Cape Hatteras Lighthouse was built, the sea has risen close to its foundations, several times nearly toppling the structure. However, due to human efforts or natural processes, the sea has recently given this monument a reprieve.

Today the Intracoastal Waterway is less the commercial channel conceived by its congressional promoters than the Southeast Coast's most popular recreational boating thoroughfare, with tens of thousands of boats using it annually.

A spider's web sparkles with dew near a tributary of the Neuse River. These freshwater droplets are part of the great water cycle which includes the rain, the rivers, the salt marshes, and the sea itself.

Although more than several hundred species of birds, including endangered raptors like the bald eagle and peregrine falcon, are found on the North Carolina coast, this area is best known for its waterfowl and waterfowling.

Above: The bridge over Oregon Inlet is the only link between Nags Head and Waves, Salvo, and other towns down the Banks. Oregon Inlet itself is the vital link between Croatan Sound and the Atlantic Ocean. *Overleaf:* Dense stands of bulrush, spikerush, panic grass, and millet rim the shores of Lake Mattamuskeet. The lake is a recent geological phenomenon.

A butterfly folds its wings on a stalk of goldenrod in Holly Shelter Swamp across the sound from Topsail Beach. The coast's fertility is a result of freshwater streams and bayous interfacing with salt water, thus creating ideal wildlife habitats.

Above: Site of the pirate Blackbeard's execution in 1718, Ocracoke Island is today the terminus of two mainland ferries at Ocracoke Village. A free ferry regularly travels north to Hatteras Island. *Overleaf:* A flight of brown pelicans cruises over the surf off Cape Lookout National Seashore. This formerly endangered species has made a notable comeback all along the Southeast Coast.

Pine barrels, packed with prime tobacco and weighing more than nine hundred pounds each, await shipment from New Bern, North Carolina. Locally produced tobacco and hogsheads have been shipped from this area for two hundred years.

A lone surf fisherman wades out to cast near Fort Fisher at the mouth of the Cape Fear River. Each spring and fall, voracious schools of bluefish push baitfish inshore, sometimes up onto the beaches. Today, the bluefish is a premier game fish of the Southeast Coast, providing excitement and food for anglers.

The lush fecundity of the shallow sea and shore merges in this tidal creek near Little River, South Carolina. Only two species of the marsh grass *Spartina* can tolerate the twice-daily inundation of salty waters. Without this grass, the coastline long ago would have eroded inland for many miles.

The state tree of South Carolina, the palmetto palm was used in the breastworks and walls of Charleston's Fort Moultrie, absorbing the bombardment by a British fleet on June 28, 1776. The successful defense of this partly completed fort was one of the first patriot victories during the American Revolution.

Off-the-beach recreation includes water slides for the kids and golf for the parents at Myrtle Beach, the heart of South Carolina's Grand Strand.

Today, the sun-worshiping population of Myrtle Beach peaks at 350,000, but before the 1920s this beach was used mostly by nesting sea turtles and birds.

The Port of Charleston is South Carolina's busiest harbor. From the Battery, once the site of some of the settlement's earliest fortifications, generations of Charlestonians have spent leisurely afternoons watching ships and people.

Murrells Inlet is the angling and seafood capital of the Grand Strand. Its fishing fleet runs up to forty miles offshore daily for king mackerel, red snapper, and black sea bass to supply the area's many popular seafood restaurants.

A great egret preens on a freshwater pond near a salt marsh in Huntington Beach State Park, which lies between Myrtle Beach and Georgetown, South Carolina.

A brown pelican poses atop its nest at the sixty thousand-acre Cape Romain National Wildlife Refuge. Twenty miles northeast of Charleston, the refuge is accessible by boat for nature study, wildlife observations, and fishing.

Founded as a plantation in the 1670s, Magnolia Gardens near Charleston is a show place for azaleas of every variety. Although most of the brilliantly flowered varieties were developed in China and Japan, all azaleas — but especially the native white azalea or swamp honeysuckle, *Rhododendron viscosa* — seem to thrive in the damp, acidic soils of the Southeast Coast.

Above: Sister Lizzie Smalls weaves a Gulah basket of sweet grass, rush, palmetto fronds, and pine needles alongside Highway 17 near Mt. Pleasant. *Overleaf:* The U.S.S. *Yorktown* (CV-10) is as much the pride of Patriots Point Naval and Maritime Museum as it was during World War II. Her planes punished the enemy at Turk, the Marianas, the Philippines, Iwo Jima, and Okinawa.

Whelks and sand dollars are the most abundant beachcombing treasures on South Carolina's barrier islands. The best time to find windrows of new shells along the beach is immediately after a major coastal storm.

Above: The most popular forms of beach-related recreation along the Grand Strand are fishing, swimming, and people-watching. *Overleaf:* Founded as an English colony in 1670, Charleston is situated on a peninsula formed by the Cooper and Ashley rivers. It is the official state port and is noted for its splendid harbor, which accommodates international and coastal commerce.

Above: Members of the North Carolina Dance Theater appear at the Spoleto Festival, Charleston's nationally acclaimed counterpart to the annual festival of the performing arts which originated in Spoleto, Italy. *Right:* Jessica Carter swims in one of the pools for guests on Seabrook Island. This island's exclusive atmosphere is very different from the more rambunctious resorts of the Grand Strand.

Left: With its economy based on rice, the heart of Middleton Place Plantation from 1741 to 1865 was this mill overlooking the Ashley River, a prime transportation corridor for the fabled rice production of the Carolinas. *Above:* Mount Pleasant's Shem Creek has long been a safe haven for numerous commercial fishing boats and a mecca for visiting gourmands.

Above: The Windswept Villas of Kiawah Island are part of a ten thousand-acre resort representing thoughtful cooperation between developer and conservationist. *Right:* A tidal pool on Capers Island reflects the late afternoon sun on fallen timber. *Overleaf:* Ten miles of wide, unspoiled beaches entice guests to take an early morning stroll on Kiawah Island.

Left: Once used extensively for bedding and packing, Spanish moss *(Tillandsia usneoides)* is a tree-borne member of the pineapple family. *Above:* The 18th hole of Hilton Head's Harbour Town golf links on the last day of the Heritage Golf Classic is a time of tension for spectators and competitors alike. *Overleaf:* The Family Circle Magazine Cup tournament, held annually at Sea Pines Racquet Club, attracts the world's top female tennis professionals.

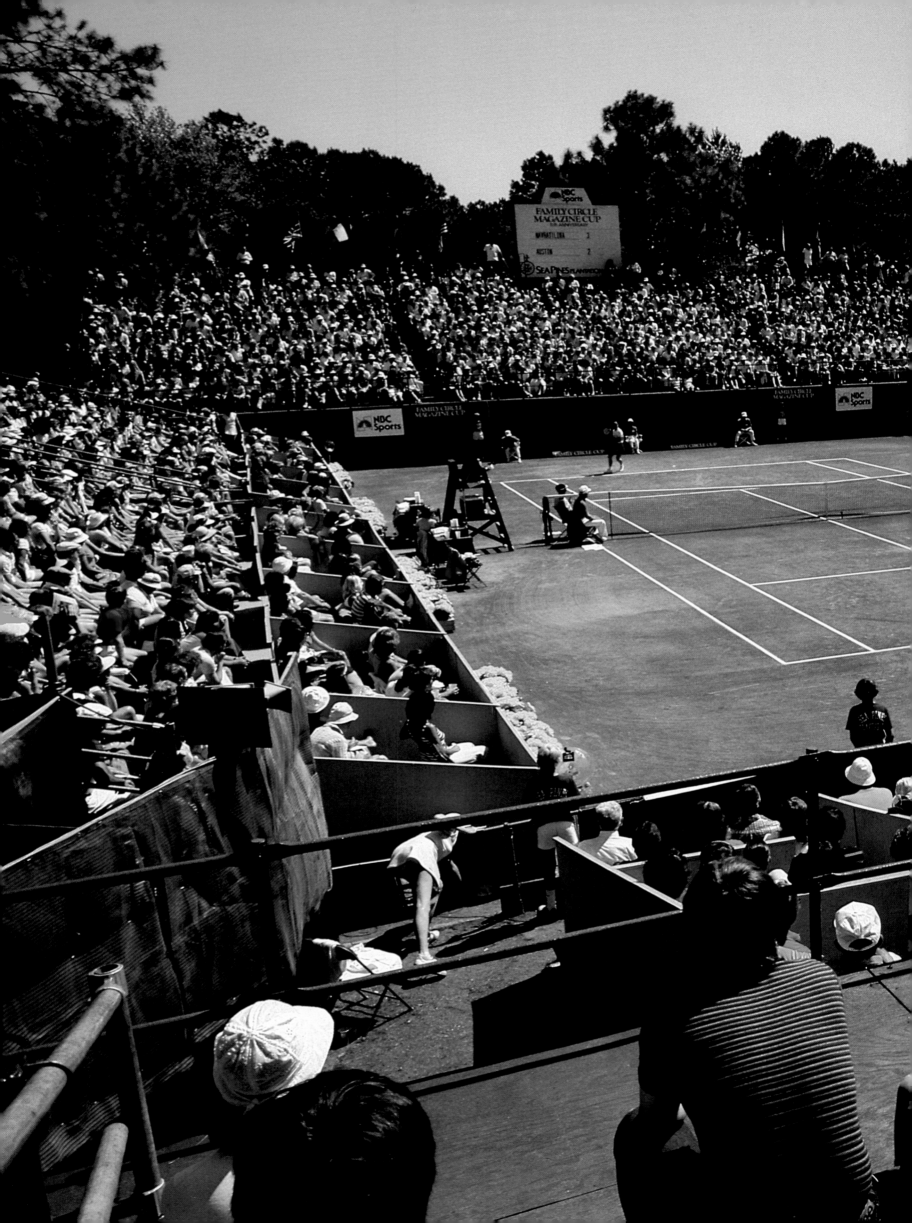

Above: Although relatively new, the coastal golf course of Wild Dunes on the Isle of Palms, near Charleston, is already considered one of the country's top courses. *Right:* The constant movement of all barrier beaches is dramatized by this palm, which has fallen across a sand-polished oak on Capers Island. *Overleaf:* When Union soldiers approached, John Drayton signaled that his house was a hospital for smallpox victims, thus saving Drayton Hall from the fires of the Union army.

Left: Fog shrouds a "boneyard beach" of trees which have succumbed to the sea on state-owned Capers Island. *Above:* Balconies overlooking the Battery are emblems both of Charleston's charm and the generations of women who have watched and waited for the return of their seafaring men.

The grace and beauty of southern living and traditional architecture are reflected in Colonial Lake, located in Charleston's three hundred-year-old historic area.

A standing sentinel guards fallen comrades, mute testimony to the eternal wearing of sea, wind, and ever-shifting sands on South Carolina's barrier islands.

The Harbour Town Lighthouse and Yacht Basin on Hilton Head Island are emblems of South Carolina's more luxurious associations with the Atlantic.

Above: Hilton Head Island is one of the premier resorts and residential communities of the Southeast Coast. *Overleaf:* Once persecuted, the alligator is now a respected symbol of the coastal low country. This ten-footer lies half submerged in the Savannah National Wildlife Refuge on the South Carolina-Georgia border.

The Indians—and the colonists after them—often built their coastal settlements on high ground overlooking oyster beds along tidal creeks and flats.

Above: A fallen frond and driftwood form a short-lived barrier against the shifting sands of a beach on Bulls Island in Cape Romain National Wildlife Refuge. *Overleaf:* A boardwalk to the sea protects the dunes from the erosion caused by trampling feet on Cumberland Island National Seashore.

A dock along the Intracoastal Waterway offers a haven to a sailboat moving north with the spring. This toll-free waterway, authorized by Congress in 1919, stimulated the economy of the Southeast Coast and was eventually expanded from Gloucester, Massachusetts, to Brownsville, Texas.

Built in 1841, Sorrel-Weed House looks across Madison Square, one of many beautiful parks in General James Edward Oglethorpe's far-sighted plan for the historic city that became an important seaport and, ultimately, modern Savannah.

Savannah's City Hall was built in 1904 on the same site as the old City Exchange, which was erected in 1794 and served throughout the era of King Cotton.

The crisp yet warming breezes of spring bring out boaters and fishers near Tybee Lighthouse, which was built in 1773 to replace a more primitive lighthouse erected under the direction of General Oglethorpe.

Trey Parrish enjoys the South's largest and most enthusiastic St. Patrick's Day celebration, when over one hundred thousand visitors crowd Savannah's streets.

Georgia's extensive salt marshes and estuaries are a nursery for many forms of sea
life which are harvested by both the people and the birds living on Tybee Island.

Virgin stands of live oak still grow in the Blackbeard Island National Wilderness Area. Used as a quarantine station for yellow fever after the Civil War and by the U.S. Navy as a source of wood for ship building in the 1800s, the island, plus its surrounding salt marshes and sea, was proclaimed the Blackbeard Island National Wildlife Refuge in 1940.

With restricted human access, the Wassaw Island National Wildlife Refuge provides a protected haven for thousands of migratory nesting birds. Here hungry young egrets wait patiently for their parents to return with food.

When the ever-present ocean breeze picks up later in the day, blowing sand will obliterate the tracks left by a foraging fox on Little St. Simons Island.

The saw or dwarf palmetto *(Sabal minor)* is the most abundant native palm along the Southeast Coast. Most commonly found in dense patches on sandy soils, it occasionally grows into a tree twenty-five feet tall.

The salt water marshes of Glynn County in southern Georgia are as soul-stirring today as they were to poet Sidney Lanier writing more than a century ago: *Ye marshes, how candid and simple and nothing-withholding and free / Ye publish yourselves to the sky and offer yourselves to the sea!*

A kestrel, North America's smallest falcon, surveys a clearing near Savannah. More commonly known as a sparrow hawk, this bird of prey thrives on insects, small rodents, and occasional small birds.

The Cloister on Sea Island blends Spanish elegance with Southern hospitality in one of the world's most distinguished hotels.

Above: Instruction in tennis, golf, horseback riding, and shooting are all available at Sea Island. *Overleaf:* Cumberland Island National Seashore is only forty-five minutes from the mainland by boat but it is light-years away in unsullied solitude. The cries of birds and the sighing of surf provide music for hikes along Cumberland's sixteen miles of beach and sand dunes.

A small bird searches for breakfast in the quiet of early morning on one of the gateways to Georgia's Golden Isles. Tens of thousands of visitors enjoy the state's natural areas and refuges, inhabited by songbirds of every type.

After a week of working off the Georgia coast, two shrimpers rest for the night at Jekyll Island. Commercial fishing is an integral part of Brunswick's economy.

Above: Built as a buffer to Spanish ambition in Florida, General Oglethorpe's Fort Frederica was the most costly British fortification in North America. In 1736 it supported a community of over one thousand people. *Right:* Jekyll Island Club House, built in 1887, was the social center for a vacation village where prominent families such as the Goodyears, Rockefellers, Morgans, and Macys assembled.

Left: Sugar-white sands of Cumberland Island gradually swallow saw palmettos, while salt-laden fog drifts across the dunes. *Above:* The power of the sea and the wild beauty of birds inspire a leisurely ride in the surf at Sea Island, Georgia.

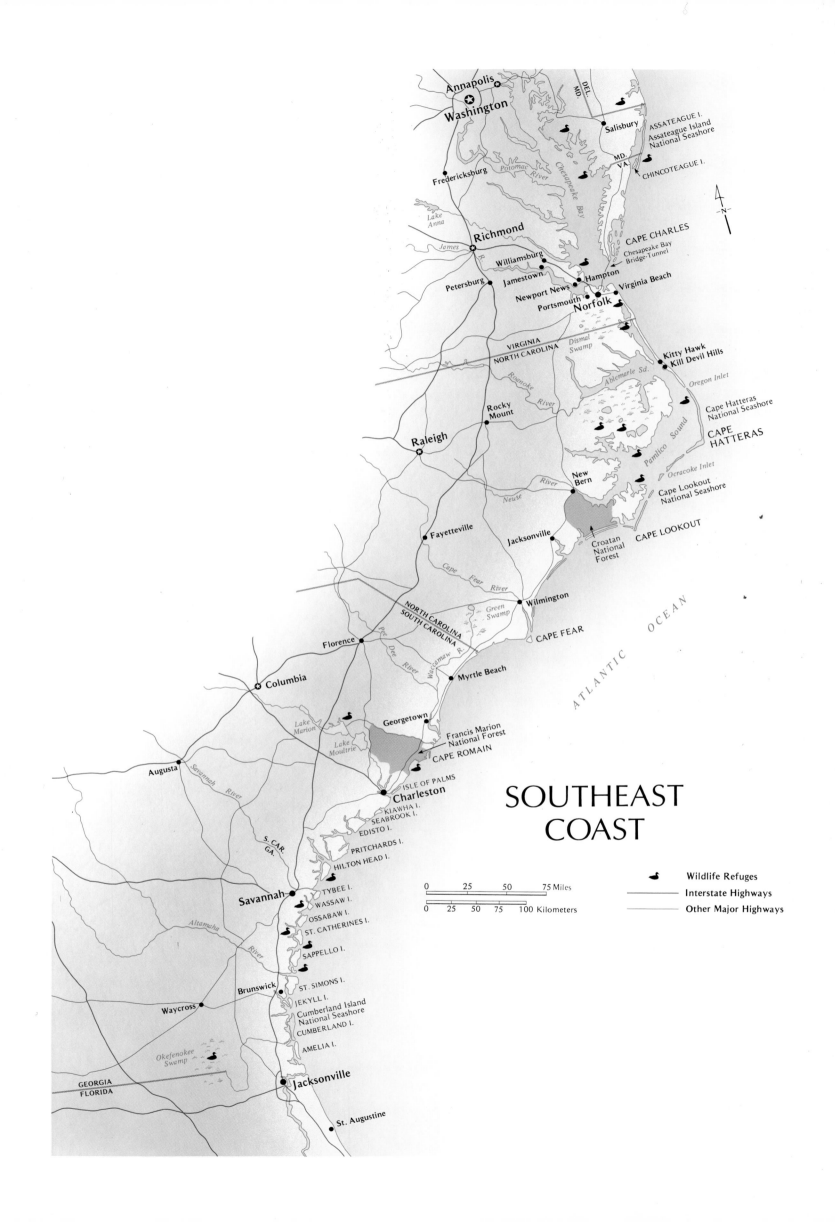

SOUTHEAST COAST

Annapolis
Washington
Fredericksburg
Richmond
Williamsburg
Petersburg
Jamestown
Newport News
Portsmouth
Hampton
Norfolk
Virginia Beach

Salisbury

ASSATEAGUE I.
Assateague Island
National Seashore

CHINCOTEAGUE I.

CAPE CHARLES
Chesapeake Bay
Bridge-Tunnel

MD.
DEL.
MD.
VA.

Chesapeake Bay

Potomac River

Lake Anna

James River

VIRGINIA
NORTH CAROLINA

Dismal Swamp

Kitty Hawk
Kill Devil Hills

Albemarle Sd.

Oregon Inlet

Cape Hatteras
National Seashore

CAPE HATTERAS

Roanoke River

Rocky Mount

Raleigh

Pamlico Sound

Ocracoke Inlet

New Bern

Cape Lookout
National Seashore

Neuse River

Croatan
National Forest

CAPE LOOKOUT

Fayetteville

Jacksonville

Cape Fear River

NORTH CAROLINA
SOUTH CAROLINA

Green Swamp

Wilmington

CAPE FEAR

ATLANTIC OCEAN

Florence

Pee Dee River

Waccamaw R.

Myrtle Beach

Columbia

Lake Marion

Lake Moultrie

Georgetown

Francis Marion
National Forest

CAPE ROMAIN

Augusta

Savannah River

ISLE OF PALMS
Charleston
KIAWHA I.
SEABROOK I.
EDISTO I.

PRITCHARDS I.

S. CAR.
GA.

HILTON HEAD I.

Savannah

TYBEE I.
WASSAW I.
OSSABAW I.
ST. CATHERINES I.

Altamaha River

SAPPELLO I.

Brunswick

ST. SIMONS I.

Waycross

JEKYLL I.
Cumberland Island
National Seashore
CUMBERLAND I.

Okefenokee
Swamp

AMELIA I.

GEORGIA
FLORIDA

Jacksonville

St. Augustine

| 0 | 25 | 50 | 75 Miles |

| 0 | 25 | 50 | 75 | 100 Kilometers |

Wildlife Refuges
Interstate Highways
Other Major Highways